PRIVACY IN THE DIGITAL AGE

SURVEILLANCE

BY A.W. BUCKEY

CONTENT CONSULTANT
M. E. Kabay, PhD, CISSP-ISSMP
Professor of Computer Information Systems
Norwich University

Cover image: Security cameras are a type of surveillance.

Core Library
An Imprint of Abdo Publishing
abdobooks.com

abdocorelibrary.com

Published by Abdo Publishing, a division of ABDO, PO Box 398166, Minneapolis, Minnesota 55439.

Printed in the United States of America, North Mankato, Minnesota
022019
092019

Cover Photo: Sunshine Studio/Shutterstock Images
Interior Photos: Sunshine Studio/Shutterstock Images, 1; Rena Schild/Shutterstock Images, 4–5, 45; Mary Altaffer/AP Images, 7; Shutterstock Images, 10; Bettmann/Getty Images, 12–13; iStockphoto, 15; Andrey Popov/Shutterstock Images, 18; Peter Thomson/La Crosse Tribune/ AP Images, 20–21, 43; Red Line Editorial, 24, 33; Joshua Lott/Reuters/Newscom, 26; Patrick Kovarik/AFP/Getty Images, 28–29; People Images/iStockphoto, 31; Thannaree Deepul/ Shutterstock Images, 34–35; Ng Han Guan/AP Images, 38–39

Editor: Maddie Spalding
Series Designer: Megan Ellis

Library of Congress Control Number: 2018966010

Publisher's Cataloging-in-Publication Data

Names: Buckey, A. W., author.
Title: Surveillance / by A. W. Buckey
Description: Minneapolis, Minnesota: Abdo Publishing, 2020 | Series: Privacy in the digital age | Includes online resources and index.
Identifiers: ISBN 9781532118944 (lib. bdg.) | ISBN 9781532173127 (ebook) | ISBN 9781644940853 (pbk.)
Subjects: LCSH: Electronic surveillance--United States--Juvenile literature. | Unauthorized interception of communications--Juvenile literature. | Data protection--Law and legislation--Juvenile literature. | Privacy, Right of--United States--Juvenile literature.
Classification: DDC 363.325163097--dc23

CONTENTS

CHAPTER ONE

We The People NOT See The People
No Spying ON AMERICA
STOP MASS SPYING
stopwatching.us
STOP MASS
FEND
TITUTIONAL
GHTS
STOPWATCHING.US

SNOWDEN'S DISCOVERY

In June 2013, a secret came out. The *Guardian* newspaper published a story from Edward Snowden. Snowden worked for a company that helped the US government. He gathered information about national security. Snowden had found secret documents. These documents worried him. He learned that the US National Security Agency

In October 2013, many people gathered in Washington, DC, to protest government surveillance.

(NSA) was monitoring people's phone calls and emails. The NSA ordered the phone company Verizon to turn over all of its phone records. The agency also used a program called PRISM. This program helped the NSA monitor internet searches. It collected information from private emails too. The NSA's goal was to find terrorists. But the NSA did not focus on just a few suspects. It investigated millions of people.

Most people had no idea the government was watching them. Snowden believed that

UK SURVEILLANCE

Snowden's leak also exposed surveillance in the United Kingdom. Some documents revealed a UK surveillance program. It was called Tempora. Tempora accessed cables that carry internet data. It captured data as it came into and out of the United Kingdom. It searched the data for important words. The UK government shared this information with the NSA. In 2017 some civil rights groups sued UK intelligence agencies. They asked these agencies to end Tempora. The European Court of Human Rights ruled that the surveillance violated people's privacy. But it said the program was not illegal.

At a news conference in 2016, human rights groups asked the US president to pardon Edward Snowden.

had to change. He thought the public had a right to know about the government's actions.

Snowden illegally downloaded secret documents. The documents showed how the NSA monitored people. He shared the documents with journalists at the *Guardian*. In 2014 the US government charged him with spying. He now lives in Russia. He continues to work on privacy issues. The information he shared sparked an ongoing debate about government surveillance.

PERSPECTIVES
BARACK OBAMA

US President Barack Obama was surprised by Snowden's decision to share secret information. Obama said that Snowden's leak "raised legitimate concerns" about surveillance. The president had the power to pardon Snowden. Then Snowden would not have been punished for his crime. But Obama decided not to pardon Snowden. He believed Snowden was wrong to break the law. Obama also argued that some surveillance was necessary for US safety.

DATA COLLECTION

The NSA collected a great deal of metadata. Data is information that can be stored and studied. Metadata is data about data. The author of the data and when it was created are examples of metadata. The NSA usually did not collect the actual data of the phone conversations. It did not pay attention to the words spoken. Instead it collected information about the conversation.

It recorded each caller's name. It also recorded the time of a conversation. These details can give important information. The length of a phone call can show how well the callers know each other. People who spend a long time talking likely know each other well. By the end of 2012, one NSA program had collected 1 trillion metadata records. The country was under surveillance.

WHAT IS SURVEILLANCE?

Surveillance is the act of carefully observing something or someone. Surveillance is usually secret. People who are under surveillance may not be aware they are being watched.

Surveillance can be used by one person on another person. But it is more often used by organizations. Governments, companies, and police departments use surveillance. These organizations gather information on many people. This information can include a person's location or internet search history. Some organizations also surveil people's communications.

In China, street cameras capture images of people who cross streets illegally.

Today, there are many ways to surveil people. Some people think surveillance makes them safer. Others see it as a way to improve businesses. Still others think surveillance threatens people's right to privacy.

STRAIGHT TO THE SOURCE

In 2013 journalist Glenn Greenwald interviewed Edward Snowden. Snowden talked about how he thought NSA surveillance had gone too far. He said:

> *NSA and [the] intelligence community in general is focused on getting intelligence wherever it can by any means possible. . . . Originally we saw that focus very narrowly tailored as foreign intelligence gathered overseas. Now increasingly we see that it's happening domestically and to do that they, the NSA specifically, targets the communications of everyone. It ingests them by default. It collects them in its system and it filters them and it analyzes them. . . . So while they may be intending to target someone associated with a foreign government or someone they suspect of terrorism, they're collecting your communications to do so.*

Source: Gabriel Rodriguez. "Edward Snowden Interview Transcript." *Mic*. Mic Network, June 9, 2013. Web. Accessed November 29, 2018.

Point of View

Snowden thinks that the NSA's surveillance methods are too extreme. What reasons does he give to back up his opinion? Read back through this chapter. Do you agree with Snowden? Why or why not?

CHAPTER
TWO

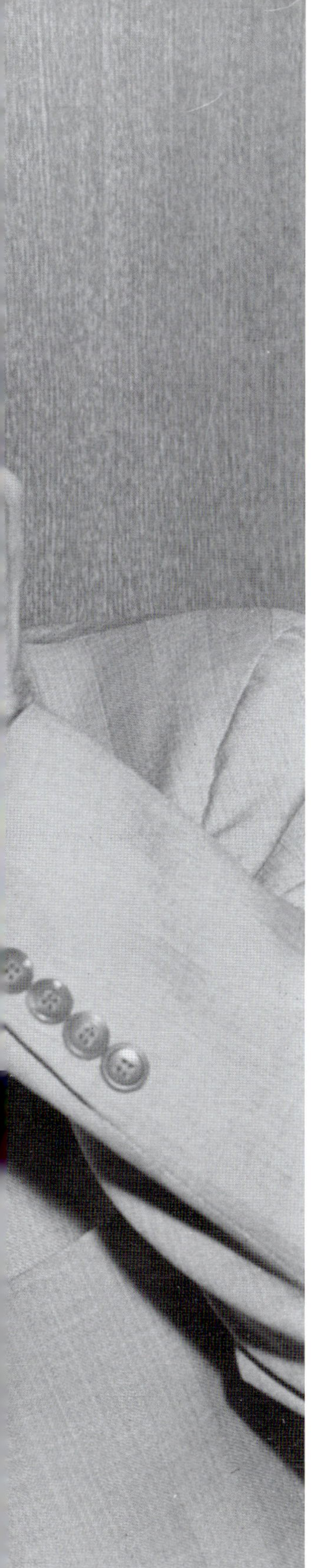

CHANGES IN SURVEILLANCE

People have been using surveillance for thousands of years. Technology has made surveillance easier and more common. The history of modern surveillance began in the 1800s.

WIRETAPPING

The electric telegraph was invented in the mid-1800s. It allowed people to send messages called telegrams. Telegrams were sent as electrical signals along wires. Some people found a way to intercept other people's telegrams. They could attach their own wires to the telegraph lines. This type of

In the early and mid-1900s, people developed equipment to wiretap telephones.

surveillance was called wiretapping. Soldiers in the American Civil War (1861–1865) used wiretapping to learn about their enemies' plans.

The first telephones also used wires to carry electrical signals. Some large companies wiretapped phones to spy on employees. Private detectives used wiretapping to spy on people. In 1928 the US Supreme Court said it was legal to wiretap people without their knowledge. In 1967 the court changed its opinion. It ruled that people need to get a warrant

PERSPECTIVES

HISTORIAN BRIAN HOCHMAN

Brian Hochman is a professor and historian. He studies the history of surveillance. He wrote a book about wiretapping. He discovered that wiretapping was used by companies before it was used by governments. Surveillance has been a part of American life for more than 100 years. But it is not always talked about. Hochman said, "Americans have come to terms with the inconvenient truth that there is no such thing as electronic communication without electronic eavesdropping."

"All the News That's Fit to Print"

The New York Times

LATE CITY EDITION

VOL. CXXIII....No. 42,566

NEW YORK, FRIDAY, AUGUST 9, 1974

15 CENTS

NIXON RESIGNS

HE URGES A TIME OF 'HEALING'; FORD WILL TAKE OFFICE TODAY

'Sacrifice' Is Praised; Kissinger to Remain

By ANTHONY RIPLEY

The 37th President Is First to Quit Post

By JOHN HERBERS

SPECULATION RIFE ON VICE PRESIDENT

POLITICAL SCENE SHARPLY ALTERED

Rise and Fall

Appraisal of Nixon Career

JAWORSKI ASSERTS NO DEAL WAS MADE

After the discovery that Richard Nixon was behind the Watergate scandal, Nixon resigned.

to wiretap. Warrants are documents that give people authority to do something.

WATERGATE

In 1972 President Richard Nixon was up for reelection. He hired a group of burglars. The burglars broke into the Democratic National Headquarters. They wiretapped phones in the office. Nixon wanted to learn about his opponents. Police arrested the burglars. The Federal Bureau of Investigation (FBI) later discovered that Nixon was behind the scheme. This event was called the Watergate scandal. In 1978 the Foreign Intelligence Surveillance Act was passed. This act required the government to get permission from a special court to surveil citizens.

MODERN SURVEILLANCE

In the 1990s, the internet became popular. Website owners could make money by selling advertising space. Today, many sites have advertisements. Some companies surveil their users to figure out where to place online ads. This surveillance involves collecting data. For example, Facebook collects data about the posts its users like and share. This data helps Facebook learn about people's interests. Then Facebook can figure out which ads a user may like. Advertisers pay Facebook to show ads. Ads that are designed for a specific group of people are called targeted ads.

Social media sites such as Facebook can be used for surveillance in other ways too. Police and the government sometimes look at social media profiles. They can use these profiles to find a person's location and interests. Police can use this information to track down a suspect.

Another invention that made surveillance easier is the Global Positioning System (GPS). GPS sends and receives signals. Satellites send these signals. Control stations on the ground contact satellites. GPS devices use signals from the satellites to determine the device's location. GPS technology became available to the public in 1993. The US government runs the satellites and control stations.

GPS SURVEILLANCE

The US government says that phone surveillance is used to fight crime and terrorism. But it can be used to surveil innocent people. For example, Yasir Afifi found a GPS tracker underneath his car in 2011. The FBI had put the tracker there. The FBI did not have a warrant to track him. Afifi was not a criminal. He believed the FBI targeted him because he is a Muslim. Afifi brought his case to court but lost.

People often use GPS devices to get directions.

GPS can be used to surveil people. For example, criminal suspects are sometimes not allowed to travel long distances. They may be required to wear GPS trackers. GPS trackers record their movements.

Mobile devices often connect to the internet. They also have GPS chips. Smartphones are common surveillance targets. It is possible to find a mobile phone's location using cell phone towers. A cell phone sends signals to nearby towers. A signal hitting a tower is called a ping. Cell phone companies keep track of which towers a phone pings. This information can be used to track a phone's location.

EXPLORE ONLINE

Chapter Two talks about the history of surveillance. The article at the website below goes into more depth on this topic. As you know, every source is different. What information does the website give about this topic? How is the information from the website the same as the information in Chapter Two? What new information did you learn from the website?

A WORLD HISTORY OF GOVERNMENT SPYING

abdocorelibrary.com/surveillance

CHAPTER
THREE

GOVERNMENT SURVEILLANCE

Many governments collect information about possible threats. This information is called intelligence. Governments use intelligence to strategize against enemies. But governments also must protect their citizens' rights. One important right is the right to privacy.

Some police departments use drones to surveil people.

PERSPECTIVES

TARGETED BY THE GOVERNMENT

Faisal Gill is a lawyer and politician. He worked in the Department of Homeland Security (DHS) from 2001 to 2005. The DHS monitors possible threats to the United States. Gill handled top-secret information. He learned that the NSA surveilled him from 2006 to 2008. The NSA read his private emails. Gill was surprised to learn he had been surveilled. "I've done everything in my life to be patriotic," he said. Gill believes he was targeted because he is a Muslim. Many other Muslims were surveilled during this time period. Anti-Muslim prejudice increased after the September 11 terrorist attacks. The terrorists involved in those attacks were Muslim.

On September 11, 2001, terrorists hijacked US airliners and crashed them into buildings in New York and Virginia. Nearly 3,000 people died. The US government called for greater surveillance powers. It wanted to prevent future attacks. Some people argue that this surveillance interferes with people's right to privacy.

THE USA PATRIOT ACT

In 2001 the US Congress passed a law commonly called

the USA PATRIOT Act. The word "patriot" has a positive meaning for many people. Congress hoped this name would make people feel positively about the law. The law was a response to the September 11 attacks. It gave intelligence agencies new surveillance powers. One section of the law was especially important. It was called Section 215. It allowed the government to give a secret order to any business. The order would force the business to give information about its customers. Section 215 also allowed the NSA

THE FOURTH AMENDMENT

The Fourth Amendment is part of the US Constitution. It says that the government and police cannot search people without good reason. They are not allowed to search people's property without cause. Surveillance laws are based in this amendment. Some digital data is considered property. For example, law enforcement must get a warrant before searching cell phone records. But there are exceptions to this rule. The government can collect foreign intelligence data without a warrant.

NSA PHONE SURVEILLANCE

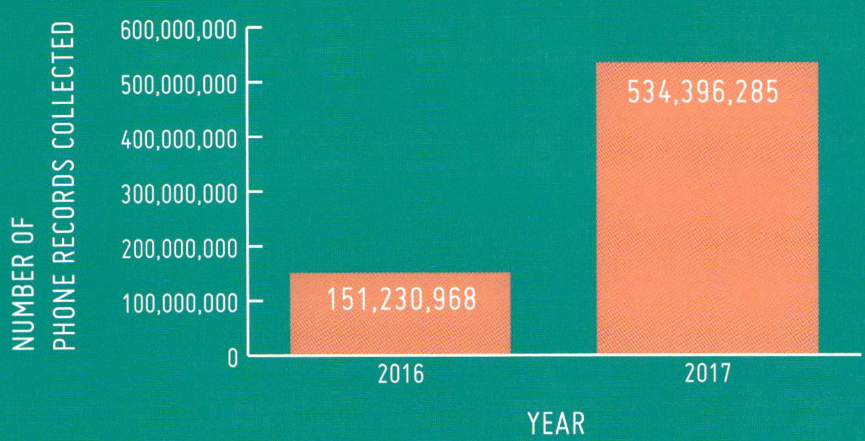

The NSA collected nearly 5 billion phone records each day in 2013. The number of records the NSA collects has decreased since then, but it still remains high. The above graph shows the number of phone records the NSA collected in 2016 and 2017. Why do you think the NSA increased its data collection in these years?

to collect phone records. The government hoped this surveillance would help catch terrorists.

Section 215 has been debated since the USA PATRIOT Act was passed. Many people thought that businesses should be able to keep their information private. Section 215 stopped being law in 2015. The number of records the NSA collects has decreased since 2013. Still, it remains high. The number of records collected increased from 2016 to 2017. Some people are concerned about this increase.

SURVEILLANCE AND POLICE

Police departments use surveillance to help prevent crime. For example, the Los Angeles Police Department (LAPD) collects data. This data includes the times and locations of previous crimes. The police study this data. They increase patrolling in areas where they predict crimes will occur. The LAPD says this technique makes policing more effective. But some people say it increases the surveillance of innocent people.

The LAPD also plans to use drones. Drones are machines that fly without pilots. People use remotes to control drones. Surveillance drones have cameras. They fly above neighborhoods. They record pictures and videos. The LAPD says it will follow strict rules with the use of these drones. Critics believe these drones will interfere with residents' privacy.

Some police departments require officers to wear body cameras.

Another police surveillance technology is body cameras. Body cameras are cameras placed on an officer. They surveil officers and suspects. More than 30 US states have body-camera laws. Police officers wear body cameras while on duty. The camera records the officer's actions. Some people think these cameras will help prevent police violence. They say that cameras can make officers more aware of their actions. But some people have concerns. Victims or witnesses of crimes may not want to be recorded. Recent research shows that body cameras do not change the way police behave.

FURTHER EVIDENCE

Chapter Three discusses the USA PATRIOT Act. What was one of the main points of this chapter? What evidence is included to support this point? The website at the link below also discusses the USA PATRIOT Act. Find a quote on this website that supports the main point you identified. Does the quote support an existing piece of evidence in the chapter? Or does it offer a new piece of evidence?

THE USA PATRIOT ACT

abdocorelibrary.com/surveillance

CHAPTER FOUR

PRIVATE SURVEILLANCE

Private companies also use surveillance. Their methods are similar to the methods used by the US government. But their goals are different. Private surveillance can be a way to control employees. Companies also use surveillance to watch and research customers.

CUSTOMER SURVEILLANCE

Many companies use closed-circuit television (CCTV) technology. This technology is used in video surveillance. It allows video footage from a security camera to be viewed

Security guards use video surveillance to watch for threats.

on a screen. It is legal to install security cameras in most public places. Security guards in stores use security cameras to watch customers. They make sure customers are not stealing goods.

It is also common for companies to surveil customers online. Private websites often use cookies. A computer downloads cookies when a user visits a website. Cookies record information about the sites a person visits. The cookies report that information to the website they

FACIAL RECOGNITION

Technology and retail company Amazon has a surveillance technology called Rekognition. It can be used by police departments. It applies facial recognition to images and videos. Facial recognition software maps people's faces. It can identify people. Rekognition compares its facial recognition to databases to identify people. Amazon says this technology would help police find suspects. But the technology still has flaws. It is less likely to correctly identify the faces of people of color. This flaw could lead to more racial bias in arrests.

Cookies track the websites people visit.

came from. This may be the website of a certain company. Cookies remember information. This allows people to easily find and access sites they have visited before. Cookies also help companies. Companies use cookies to understand customers' spending habits. They use this information to market themselves. For example, a company that sells kitchen supplies could use tracking cookies. These cookies might follow customers to their favorite recipe blogs. The kitchen supply company could use that information. It could ask to advertise on those blogs.

PERSPECTIVES

ONLINE SURVEILLANCE

Ethan Zuckerman is a former website developer. He figured out how to help websites sell ads. He invented the pop-up ad. Pop-up ads are ads that appear on websites. Clicking on these ads redirects the user to the advertiser's site. Zuckerman regrets inventing pop-up ads. He knows that many users find them annoying. He also believes they helped make online surveillance widespread. He supports tougher privacy laws. He thinks people shouldn't have to accept surveillance in order to use websites.

EMPLOYEE SURVEILLANCE

Many companies surveil their employees. A company may use surveillance to monitor employee performance. For example, a company called Upwork uses surveillance. Upwork helps freelancers find jobs. Freelancers work from home. They get projects from different companies. The Upwork site has surveillance software. The software takes pictures of freelancers' computer screens. It measures how often the freelancers type on their keyboards.

SURVEILLANCE CONCERNS

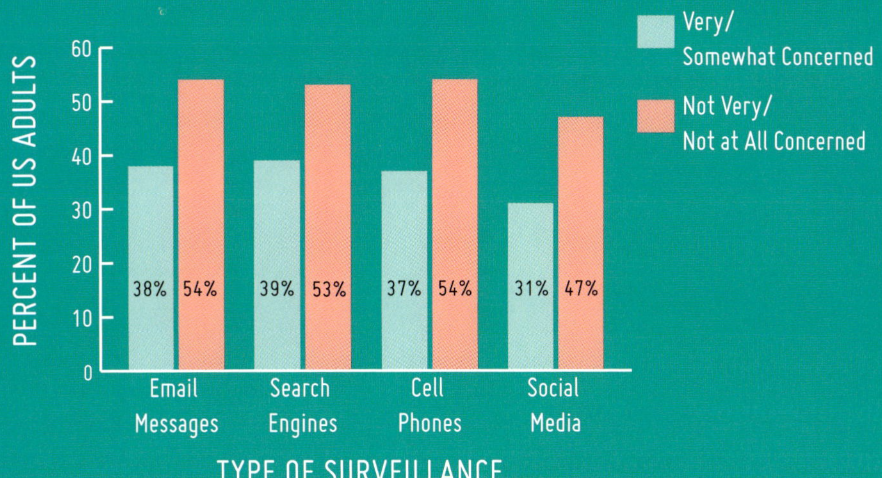

The above graph shows how concerned US adults are about government surveillance in different areas. This data comes from a 2015 survey of 475 adults. Do these numbers surprise you? Why or why not?

Many companies also surveil their workers' communications. A 2018 survey showed that 98 percent of large companies surveil their employees' computers. Employers may legally read an employee's messages if they are sent or received on company devices. Employers are required to tell their employees about these surveillance rules.

CHAPTER FIVE

THE FUTURE OF SURVEILLANCE

New technology leads to new surveillance possibilities. Drone technology has grown quickly in recent years. The LAPD is not the only police department interested in drones. In June 2018, technology company Axon announced a partnership. Axon and a drone maker will sell drones to police departments across the country.

People can buy surveillance drones online or in stores. They might use these drones to

CCTV cameras can be used to monitor traffic and make sure people follow rules.

film interesting events and scenery. But drones can also be used to spy on people.

SMART TECHNOLOGY

Smart technology uses surveillance to provide services to people. Smart devices are household objects that store data. They collect information about their users. One popular smart device is a smart fridge. These fridges have cameras inside them. The cameras can connect to a smartphone. This allows users to look inside their fridge while at the grocery store. They can see what foods they need to buy. Creators of smart devices can store and share data collected by the devices. Smart devices are part of the Internet of Things (IoT). The IoT is a network of devices that connect to the internet.

ANTI-SURVEILLANCE

Some people work on anti-surveillance strategies. These are strategies to keep information hidden. Special tools can be used to protect a person's privacy. Some people use the Pretty Good Privacy (PGP) program. This program protects private information, such as emails. It uses two keys. The keys are pieces of software. One key is called a public key. It encrypts text. Encryption makes the text unreadable. Another key is called a private key. It decrypts the text. Decryption makes text readable again. People may use a PGP program when they want to send sensitive information. The sender uses a

END-TO-END ENCRYPTION

A lot of online information is encrypted. But encrypted information sometimes becomes decrypted before it reaches its destination. People who are not meant to receive the message could intercept it. End-to-end encryption prevents this problem. This process keeps data encrypted. Information stays encrypted from the time it is sent until someone receives it. For example, the texting app WhatsApp uses end-to-end encryption. The company cannot decode messages between users as they are sent. Only senders and receivers can access the texts.

In western China, police heavily surveil Uighur communities.

public key to encrypt the message. The person who receives the message uses a private key to decrypt it.

SURVEILLANCE AND HUMAN RIGHTS

Many human rights groups are concerned about surveillance. Governments can use it to restrict people's rights. For example, the Chinese government uses surveillance cameras with facial recognition software.

This software can identify people in a crowd. The government also surveils social media accounts. It targets people who create or like anti-government posts. Police in China surveil Uighur communities. Uighurs are a Muslim minority group. In 2014 police began to arrest Uighurs and put them into camps. Today, as many as 1 million Uighurs live in these camps.

PERSPECTIVES

FOOD CART SURVEILLANCE

In July 2018, Human Rights Watch published a report on the surveillance of New York City street vendors. Street vendors sell food out of carts. The New York City government proposed a GPS tracking law for these food carts. The city said that tracking carts would make it easier for health inspectors to find them. The vendors argued that GPS tracking invades their privacy. Some vendors are undocumented immigrants. They worry that law enforcement might use their location data to track and arrest them. One vendor said, "This will harm vendors and we reject this proposal."

In the United States, widespread surveillance continues. As technology grows and changes, so do the ways that people can be watched. Surveillance has some benefits. It can help police catch criminals. It can protect stores from theft. But many people argue that surveillance violates people's right to privacy. They wonder if the benefits are worth the costs.

STRAIGHT TO THE SOURCE

Ramy Raoof is a digital security expert. In a 2017 interview, he explained how some governments abuse surveillance. He said:

> *The way [states] are using surveillance is to limit people's ability to organize. And people organize through different means: it could be through mobile apps or websites. . . . And then the adversary deploys surveillance to monitor people—not to ban them, but to know what they are going to do and then disrupt this action in some way.*
>
> *They think through surveillance they will disrupt people's ability to organize and speak freely. So when there is a group of people trying to organize a protest . . . the main way to make it ineffective is by monitoring people's lives.*

Source: Centro de Estudios Legales y Sociales. "State Surveillance and Protest." *Open Democracy*. Open Democracy, October 4, 2017. Web. Accessed November 30, 2018.

Consider Your Audience

Adapt this passage for a different audience, such as your principal or friends. Write a blog post conveying this same information for the new audience. How does your post differ from the original text and why?

FAST FACTS

- Surveillance involves spying on people to get information. Governments, companies, and people sometimes use surveillance.
- Listening to phone calls, reading private emails, and studying people's internet activity are all common types of surveillance. GPS location tracking is another common surveillance method.
- In 2013 government employee Edward Snowden released secret documents. They revealed the US government's methods of mass surveillance.
- Private companies use surveillance on employees and customers. Video surveillance is a tool to prevent theft. Companies surveil customers online in order to advertise and do research.
- Anti-surveillance technology allows people to protect their privacy. PGP and end-to-end encryption protect users' online information.
- Some people argue that government surveillance can be used to limit people's rights. They support stronger laws against private and government surveillance.

STOP AND THINK

Tell the Tale

Chapter One of this book talks about Edward Snowden's decision to share secret government information. Imagine you are in Snowden's position. Write 200 words about whether you would choose to share the information. How would you make your decision?

Say What?

Studying surveillance can mean learning a lot of new vocabulary. Find five words in this book you've never seen before. Use a dictionary to find out what they mean. Then write the meanings in your own words, and use each word in a new sentence.

Take a Stand

Some people believe that surveillance is an important security tool. Others think that surveillance invades people's privacy. What is your opinion? Do you think a government should be allowed to surveil its citizens? Do you think there should be limits to government surveillance?

Why Do I Care?

Maybe you are not interested in surveillance. But it is very possible that surveillance affects your life. How does surveillance affect the things you see online? How do you think your life might be different without surveillance?

GLOSSARY

bias
favoring certain people or points of view over others

data
information that can be stored and studied

encryption
the act of coding data so that it cannot be understood in order to keep it private

immigrant
a person who moves from one country to live in another

intelligence
information that has a useful purpose

metadata
information about data

pardon
to formally forgive someone for a crime committed

prejudice
a dislike of someone or something

terrorism
the act of using violence or threats to frighten people

warrant
an official document that gives a person the authority to do something

ONLINE RESOURCES

To learn more about surveillance, visit our free resource websites below.

Visit **abdocorelibrary.com** or scan this QR code for free Common Core resources for teachers and students, including vetted activities, multimedia, and booklinks, for deeper subject comprehension.

Visit **abdobooklinks.com** or scan this QR code for free additional online weblinks for further learning. These links are routinely monitored and updated to provide the most current information available.

LEARN MORE

Conley, Kate. *Inside Drones*. Minneapolis, MN: Abdo Publishing, 2019.

Smibert, Angie. *Inside Computers*. Minneapolis, MN: Abdo Publishing, 2019.

INDEX

About the Author

A.W. Buckey is a writer living in Brooklyn, New York.